Compass Point

Phonics Readers

Push or Pull?

by Wiley Blevins

Reading Consultant: Wiley Blevins, M.A.
Phonics/Early Reading Specialist

 COMPASS POINT BOOKS

Minneapolis, Minnesota

Compass Point Books
3109 West 50th Street, #115
Minneapolis, MN 55410

Visit Compass Point Books on the Internet at *www.compasspointbooks.com*
or e-mail your request to *custserv@compasspointbooks.com*

Editorial Development: Alice Dickstein, Alice Boynton
Photo Researcher: Wanda Winch
Design/Page Production: Silver Editions, Inc.

Library of Congress Cataloging-in-Publication Data
Blevins, Wiley.
   Push or pull? / by Wiley Blevins.
      p. cm. — (Compass Point phonics readers)
   Includes index.
   Summary: Discusses forces such as push or pull in an easy-to-read text
that incorporates phonics instruction and rebuses.
   ISBN 0-7565-0521-6 (hardcover : alk. paper)
   1. Force and energy—Juvenile literature. 2. Reading—Phonetic
method—Juvenile literature. [1. Force and energy. 2. Rebuses. 3.
Reading—Phonetic method.] I. Title. II. Series.
   QC73.4.B54 2004
   531'.6—dc21   2003006366

Table of Contents

Dear Parent or Caregiver,

Welcome to Compass Point Phonics Readers, books of information for young children. Each book concentrates on specific phonic sounds and words commonly found in beginning reading materials. Featuring eye-catching photographs, every book explores a single science or social studies concept that is sure to grab a child's interest.

So snuggle up with your child, and let's begin. Start by reading aloud the Mother Goose nursery rhyme on the next page. As you read, stress the words in dark type. These are the words that contain the phonic sounds featured in this book. After several readings, pause before the rhyming words, and let your child chime in.

Now let's read *Push or Pull?* If your child is a beginning reader, have him or her first read it silently. Then ask your child to read it aloud. For children who are not yet reading, read the book aloud as you run your finger under the words. Ask your child to imitate, or "echo," what he or she has just heard.

Discussing the book's content with your child:
Explain to your child that sometimes it's difficult to tell whether an object is moving from a push or a pull. Look at the picture on page 9. Ask your child if the ball is going to be pushed or pulled. A baseball bat hitting a ball is an example of a push. The bat pushes the ball away.

At the back of the book is a fun Word Bingo game. Your child will take pride in demonstrating his or her mastery of the phonic sounds and the high-frequency words.

Enjoy Compass Point Phonics Readers and watch your child read and learn!

4

Jenny Has a Little Mule

Jenny has a little **mule**,
It is so very **cute**,
It likes to munch on sugar **cubes**,
And sit with her in school.

But then one day that little **mule**,
Who is so very **cute**,
Began to lunch on teacher's chalk,
And drink from fishies' pool!

Jenny has a little **mule**,
It's still so very **cute**,
But now it crunches leaves and grass,
And waits outside of school.

This is a huge cube.
Can you lift it?
Can you roll it?
What will make it move?

Use a rope and pull it.
When it is pulled, the cube
is tugged close to you.

Get a few kids and push it.
When it is pushed, the cube
is pressed away from you.

A push or a pull is a force.
It is needed to make an object move.
A push presses an object away.
A pull tugs an object close.

This man plays on a team.
When he kicks the  ball ,
he pushes it with his feet.
He may kick it hard or just tap it.

If he kicks the  hard,
he uses a lot of force.
A lot of force makes it move fast.
Less force makes it move slowly.

What is needed to make the sled
move up the hill?
What is needed to make the swing
move up and back?

Word List

Long *u* (*u_e, ew*)

u_e
cube
huge
use(s)

ew
few

-ed
needed
pressed
tugged

High-Frequency
pull(ed)

Science
force
hard
push(ed), (es)
slowly

Word Bingo

Player 1

use	needed	cute
cube	few	tugged
pull	huge	new

How to Play

- Fold and cut a sheet of paper into 11 pieces. Write each game word on one of the pieces. The words are *cube, cute, few, huge, mule, needed, new, pressed, pull, tugged, use.*
- Fold each piece of paper and put it in a bag or box.
- The players take turns picking a folded paper and reading the word aloud. Each player then covers the word if it appears on his or her game card. The first player to cover 3 words either down, across, or on the diagonal wins. You can also play until the whole card is covered.

Player 2

cube	pull	new
mule	huge	use
few	cute	pressed

Read More

Bryant-Mole, Karen. *Forces*. Science All Around Me Series. Chicago, Ill.: Heinemann Library, 1997.

Royston, Angela. *Forces and Motion*. My World of Science Series. Chicago, Ill.: Heinemann Library, 2002.

Schaefer, Lola M. *Push and Pull*. The Way Things Move. Mankato, Minn.: Pebble Books, 2000.

Stewart, Melissa. *Motion*. Simply Science Series. Minneapolis, Minn.: Compass Point Books, 2003.

Waters, Jennifer. *Move It!* Minneapolis, Minn.: Compass Point Books, 2002.

Index